Spiritual Peace:
A Collection of Biblically Insp...
Adair A. Rowan

Midwest Creations Publishing & Media
St. Louis, MO 63114
Visit our website at https://midwest-creations-publishing.square.site

    This is an original work of nonfiction based on author study and life experiences.

    The information provided in this publication is not to be considered a substitute for medical advice. The authors are not physicians and do not claim to be so.

    Any use of strategies stipulated here after are considered general information and suggestions, should the reader choose to apply them it will be at their sole discretion and own risk.

    The publisher does not have any control over and does not resume responsibility for the author or any third-party (reviewers, bloggers, booksellers, social network etc.) or their content.

Spiritual Peacer:
A Collection of Biblically Inspired Writings
Adair A. Rowan

Copyright ©2023 Adair A. Rowan
ISBN-13: 978-1-7338114-9-1
ISBN-10: 978-1-733811
All rights reserved. No part of this book may be reproduced by any means (including but not limited to electronically via scanning, mechanically

printed or handwritten) nor copied or shared without the express permission in written form from the author or publisher in representation of the author; the exception being a direct quotation of a paragraph or brief passage by a reviewer or blogger.

Cover Illustration copyright ©2023 by Adair A.Rowan and Midwest Creations Publishing &MEdia, LLC. All rights reserved.

Edited by Midwest Creations Publishing & MEdia, LLC

Designed by Midwest Creations Publishing & MEdia, LLC

Printed in the United States of America

Originally published electronically via KDP by Midwest Creations Publishing & MEdia, LLC

SPIRITUAL PEACE

A Collection of Biblically Inspired Writings

Written by ADAIR A. ROWAN

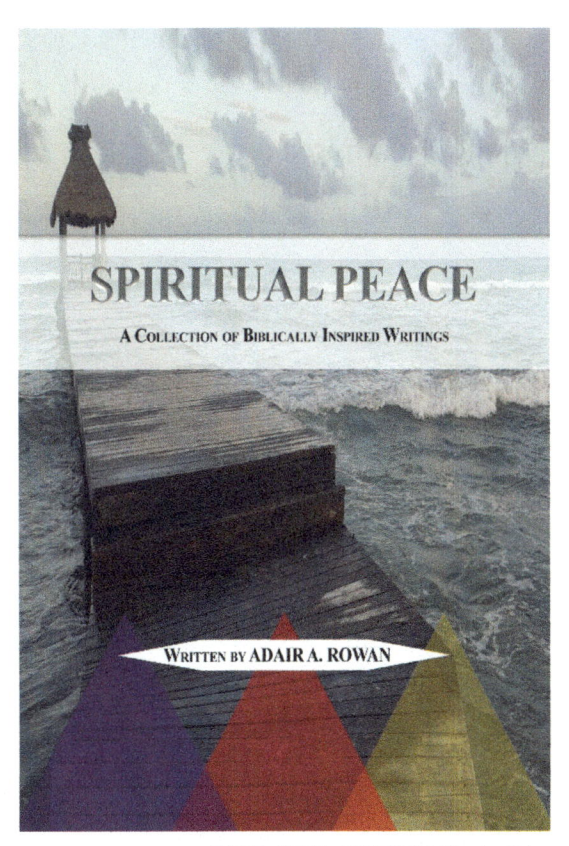

SPIRITUAL

ABSTRACT
Life can take us on many twists and turns. During our journey, we must always lean on the Word of God to give us the strength to withstand the storms of life and recognize also the times of plenty.

Adair A rowan

PEACE

A Collection of Biblically Inspired Writings

v

SPIRITUAL PEACE
A Collection of Biblically Inspired Writings

Adair A. Rowan

To my wife Allison, a precious gift from above; I thank you for your love, encouragement, and support. You're always a safe space to share thoughts and ideas. To my boys Grant and Gavin, you both are an inspiration as I strive to set a good example of fatherhood and faithfulness before you. To my brother John, aka Blue Bulldog, keep laying it on thick; you know! Wink wink. To my mother Wonder, so aptly named. You have always been a great example of an overcomer. I know as a child I gave you the blues, but you kept me in line and taught me to keep stepping forward. To my cousin Denise (if anybody has a problem with you, they can't be around me because you have one of the sweetest spirits I've ever known. To my SIL Justine, keep being the No-nonsense, but loveable you. To the greatest in-laws of all time, the Grant Family. To Chantay and Micante, thank you for the laughs and push, sometimes we all get sidetracked, but you never let me get complacent. To my brother from another mother JVN, your walk showed your faith before you confessed it my brother. In memorial of my father Ernest, the Lord granted us 7 years and one to repair and rebuild our relationship. In memory of Mama Doris, your wit was fantastic and will be missed.
Also, I would like to honor some of the Men of God that inspired this work. In honor of Reverend Ronald

Packnett (RIH); Pastor Samuel J Gilbert Sr (aka Pastor E), Pastor Carl Smith, Pastor D.Z. Cofield, and Pastor Ralph West Sr (aka Pas). Your wisdom and exposition of the Word of God have been a blessing and I pray that this work encourages other believers.

Contents

Introduction xi
I THANK THE LORD 2
JUDGING ANGELS 4
CYPHA FOR JESUS 9
I WILL NOT GIVE UP 12
I HAVE YOUR BEST INTEREST AT HEART 16
ISN'T IT FUNNY? 19
WHICH WAY DO I GO? 22
RED POEM 23
THIS CHRISTMAS 24
WHAT DO YOU BELIEVE IN? 25
GOD'S MAN 29
SO YOU CALL YOURSELF A CHRISTIAN 37
HAVE YOU LOST YOUR MIND? 43
PARTING THOUGHTS 51

INTRODUCTION

This collection of writings is inspired by the numerous sermons I have witnessed over the years. Believers, we are instructed by the Word of God in **2 Timothy 2:15** which states, "Do your best to present yourself to God as one approved, a worker who does not need to be ashamed and who correctly handles the word of truth." (NIV)

If you are in that generation who came up under the old school preachers and transitioned into the newer non-denominational idea of Christianity; the King James version says it this way, "Study to shew thyself approved unto God, a workman that needeth not to be ashamed, rightly dividing the word of truth."

I often ponder this scripture. What does it mean? How does this influence my life? -I've come to understand that **2 Timothy 2:15** is saying all of us are workmen in the kingdom. You don't need a specific title to be a workman. You only need to confess with your mouth and believe in your heart.

These are the initial things that you must do; the milk of a baby Christian. How do you strengthen the spirit man that lives within you? The spirit of Christ?

You must take in the Word through sermons, reading the scriptures, meditation on the scriptures, and prayer. There are also times when you must fast to eliminate distractions, for a better focus on what the Lord is trying to teach you or allow you to see and understand.

These writings are based on various situations in life for which I pondered the scriptures to address. Sometimes the scriptures inspired writings as they related to the various joyful celebrations on the calendar, or the dark times that I've had to deal with loss.

Much like the book of Psalms, these writings are shared in the order in which they were inspired. Sometimes, the writing was inspired by a phrase in a sermon I heard at church, other times it was a Biblical discussion or one I heard on a recorded sermon.

x

The Word can come to you and inspire you in a small storefront or a huge cathedral because the Holy Spirit cares not about the physical location, but more about the heart of the Believer, whether the Believer is aware or not of their own need at that time.

I do not claim to be a Biblical scholar. I have not attended seminary. I began my journey toward the life of a Believer at the Jehovah Witness Halls in St. Louis, MO attending with a family friend. I moved onward to Christian life at Central Baptist Church near downtown St. Louis thanks to our loving neighbors Julian and Maude Kelly. They were an awesome elderly couple who took a keen interest in our family. They invited us to church over and over again, without pressure. Eventually our whole family was baptized under Pastor Ronald Barrington Packnett. He was a man of small physical stature, yet he preached with great vigor and urgency.

Pastor Packnett has gone on to be with the Lord, but I want to take a moment to thank his wife Gwendolyn Packnett, and their children Brittany and Barrington for sharing him with us. He left an impact on our souls, therefore, we thank you and love your family for that.

I left the church for a while, due to life in general. I realized I was missing something, and eventually (with prompting from my mother), I began visiting Friendly Temple Missionary Baptist Church, located on Dr. Martin Luther King drive in St. Louis. Pastor Michael Jones preached with power and passion. He is a teaching Pastor. He can whoop with the best of them, but he is also an awesome teacher and administrator.

FTMBC grew in the few years I was there from its existing building until they took over and renovated a derelict warehouse across the street; and since my move to Texas, they have gone on to building senior homes and more.

Upon moving to Texas, I joined the Eternal Love Fellowship Church on the Northwest side of Houston, which held services at the time, in a small storefront location. It was close knit, and the people were friendly. We discussed at length various scriptures, their meaning, as well as their application. While a member there I experienced one of my worst life disappointments (not a disappointment in the church, but a personal failure).

The Pastor and First Lady (Carl & Kanita Smith), a Deacon and Deaconess (K & C Gilmore), and another member (brother Jerome Porter-RIH) came to my aid during this tumultuous time. Having never been in that situation before, it was wonderful to see and experience the agape (unselfish love of one person for another without sexual implications; brotherly love) that the Bible espouses in action.

As I grew in the Word, my wife and I chose a new church, mainly because we moved across town, and it was utterly impossible to make it to church on time and participate in various church functions.

We attended Good Hope Baptist Church under the phenomenal pastorship of D.Z. Cofield. Pastor Cofield is a brilliant teacher and preacher. He can get very deep into exposition while keeping his sermons relatable and simple.

We enjoyed amazing growth while attending Good Hope; our friend circle grew as well. Yet again, we moved clear across town and needed to find a newer church home. We became members of The Church Without Walls under the masterful teachings of a very dynamic Pastor, Ralph Douglas West, aka "Pas." Even during the pandemic of 2020-2022, "Pas," as we all call him, still served up spiritual steak and potatoes via streaming sermons on the TCWW website.

So, I wrote all of that to say, I've sat under, listened to, and studied under great leadership. They've all taught me something and helped me grow.

My hope is that you are as inspired by scripture-based sermons and the scripture directly, as I have been.

These writings are what the Word of God inspired in me as a gift through various life situations. Perhaps, after reading what God gave me, you may find it a leaping point to help you ruminate on the scriptures with a refreshed mind's eye. They may inspire you to write down what God has given you to share as a part of your testimony.

Blessings upon blessings to you the reader, the Believer and even the non-Believer.

COMFORT
(LOSS OF A YOUTH)

Today is a time that we can only speak about comfort.
Comfort, in the word of God.
For the Lord said, "suffer the little children to come unto me" (**Luke 18:16**)
Today, we must acknowledge that one little child has gone to see the Lord much sooner than expected
We must acknowledge that this child also
Has a new name, that only Jesus knows
And when Jesus calls you by the name that only He knows
It is a reason to come running
It is a reason to have joy in your heart
Psalm 23:4 reads, "Yea, though I walk through the valley of the shadow of death, I will fear no evil: for thou are with me; thy rod and staff they comfort me."
The one thing that we can take comfort in knowing, is that no
Matter what comes, no matter what we face
No matter how hard the trials and tribulations may be
We have a Source of comfort
Sometimes, it slips our minds when we are going through
Yet, we are never put on the back burner
John 14:17 reads, "But the Comforter, which is the Holy Ghost, whom the Father will send in My name, He shall teach you all things, and bring all things to your remembrance, whatsoever I have said unto you.
We were taught by Jesus that we should not be concerned with what we want
But what the Father wants
Sometimes those goals don't go hand in hand
Ultimately,
No matter how you spin it
It works out for whatever God has in store
We must realize that His plan is better than ours
We must realize that His plan is better than ours
We must also remember that His plan
Requires that we cast all our burdens on God
And accept His comfort
Psalm 94:19 reads, "In the multitude of my thoughts within me thy comforts delight my soul."
On today, we commit this broken vessel back to the Potter and we take comfort in knowing that He knows what to do with the spirit that visited us
This also lets us know that we need to focus on the glory of the Lord
Because just as this child's time was infinitesimal to us

So is our time when measured against the Lord
Isaiah 49:13 reads, "Sing, O heavens; and be joyful, O earth: and break forth into singing, O mountains; for the Lord hath comforted his people and will have mercy upon his afflicted."

(This was written after a family member's baby was stillborn. This was my first time knowing anyone personally that had this experience. I did not know what to do or say. I leaned upon the Bible to help me to be sensitive to the situation, while also trying to provide faith-based comfort and encouragement to this family member.)

I THANK THE LORD

When I awoke this morning, I thanked the Lord
When I opened my eyes and sunlight temporarily blinded me, I thanked the Lord
When I could move my eyes to look around the room, I thanked the Lord
When I was able to take a deep breath, I thanked the Lord
When I was able to move my arms and my legs, I thanked the Lord
When I was able to simply roll over on my side, I thanked the Lord
When I was able to stand upright, I thanked the Lord
As I walked to the bathroom, I thanked the Lord
As I brushed my teeth, I thanked the Lord
As the phone rang in my home, I thanked the Lord
As the voice on the other end told me the good news, I was hired; I thanked the Lord
As I look back, I noticed there were times when I did not thank the Lord
When I was in high school and got suspended for fighting
I did not thank the Lord, though things could have been worse
When I was in my early 20's and another brother pointed a gun at me but did not pull the trigger
I did not thank the Lord, even though I could have died
When I was a passenger, in a car accident and had a C5 fracture
I did not thank the Lord, though I could have been paralyzed
When I had a birthday gift, my gold necklace snatched off of my neck
I did not thank God, though the brother that robbed me could have done worse than just yank a piece of jewelry off of my neck
When I think about it, there are so many things that we take for granted today
But do you think God takes us for granted?
Do you think that God should thank us for praising Him, when He made us for this purpose?
I know that I have a lot to be thankful for: health, a marriage, a home, the ability to pay my bills, sight, hearing, breathing, thinking and many more things than I could list
So, I thank God for all these things and more
I ask you: What do you thank Him for?

1 Peter 4:11 (NIV) *If anyone speaks, they should do so as one who speaks the very words of God. If anyone serves, they should do so with the strength God provides, so that in all things God may be praised through Jesus Christ. To Him be the glory and the power for ever and ever. Amen.*

Many times, as Believers, we think of praising God, to only refer to hymns and dance. But I believe that praising God includes thanking Him, not only when big things happen, but also the little things in life. If you can't thank Him for the little things, then it's even more difficult to do so when big things happen. Why? Because as human beings we tend to think that we did it. How do you combat the "World revolves around me" mentality? By focusing on the little things. If you remember that God had to allow all of these little things to occur, in a specific order, just for you to wake up each day; it will keep one humble before God.

JUDGING ANGELS
(A meditation on **1 Corinthians 6:3**)

How do you feel today?
If you can speak, you should say blessed
If you can stand, you should be joyful
If you were able to make it here, you should say that you feel anointed by God
You have been given the ultimate gift
The Hope
The Opportunity
The Potential
Of gaining eternal life
You have the chance to be appointed as a singer in the Holy choir
You will get to praise God in a choir unlike any ever known before
You will be given the awesome burden of judging angels
The angels who have been given charge over us right now
These same angels that fight the legions of the enemy in God's name on our behalf
The angels that have stood in the way of darkness
The angels that foretold us of the coming of the Son of God
You think that you know what you are worth?
I do not think you do
Know ye not that we shall judge angels?
Husbands
How can you lead if you do not follow that One who was perfect?
If you abuse and mistreat your wife
How can you be following in the footsteps of Christ?
If you are neglecting your family
How are you living up to the greatest commandment given?
Love
If you think that leading your family is simply barking orders and expecting complete submission, you are wrong
You are supposed to lead by example
You are supposed to lead with compassion
Just as God does with us
When someone makes a mistake, you do not need to condemn them
You allow God to deal with their spirit
You don't throw stones
Especially if you live in a glass house
Wives
You may think that the Word says to submit yourselves to your husbands
To keep you underfoot
This is not what God intended

You see
In Heaven, God, Christ, and the Holy Spirit live as one being
As the truest representation of the family
This family has power
As all families are supposed to have
If they are doing what they are meant to do
They should first and foremost love one another
They should be an engine
That produces more and more love
They should be a shining example of the light that God intended families to be
Our families fall short of the mark consistently and constantly
Husbands abuse their wives and children
Husbands belittle their wives and children
Husbands rule with fear instead of love
That's not how God intended
Know ye not that we shall judge angels?
Wives tear down the position of the husband
Wives forget that they are helpers as well as helpee's
You see, the concept of on earth as it is in heaven that we speak of within the prayer we call the Lord's Prayer
It means that just as when we get to heaven, we should all be on one accord
We should be trying to be that way on earth now
No man is better than any other man
Husbands are not better than their wives
Wives are not better than their husbands
You see, once you have been joined as one
You are one
Your children are supposed to be extensions of you
If you neglect your family
You've missed the mark
Husbands and Wives
You cannot neglect your family
Do you think that God would neglect His Son, or The Holy Spirit?
He never did this
He hasn't neglected us
He has done everything possible to give us a chance except write a book
Oh, wait
HE gave us the Bible
If you study and you open your heart and mind
You will become what God wants you to be
If you study, but don't open your heart and mind
You will continue to repeat the same struggles over and over again
Until you truly receive what God wants you to receive
He said, "Cast your burdens on me."

Yet you keep carrying the burdens
You won't let them go, that's why you keep on dealing with the same thing
Know ye not, that we will judge angels?
Apparently, we just don't get it
How are we going to make it if we don't first give it over to Jesus?
How are we going to make it, if we don't first have a little talk with Jesus?
How are we going to make it if we don't first believe?
How are we going to make it, if we don't first make a change?
How are we going to make it if we're moving but aren't following our directions?
How are we going to make it if we are coasting through life with blinders on?
How can we go anywhere without first going to Jesus to get to the Father?
How can we earn a place in the Book of Life without first giving our lives over to the Word?
How can we teach others if we are not willing to humble ourselves in order to first learn?
How can we be good examples without acknowledging the only one who was perfect?
A lot of us, "*Believers*" won't make it into the kingdom
A lot of us Believers won't make it before God
A lot of us Believers won't make it to the Son because
We believe that we can take our time
We don't have time on our side
Time is only on the side of God
Time is only on the side of Jesus
Time is only on the side of the Holy Spirit
Time is only on the side of the righteous
Time is only on the side of the those who are fulfilling the Great Commission
Time is only granted to those who are truly following the teachings of the living Word
Time is the only thing
That if you take advantage of it
And learn all you can learn
And teach all you can teach
And lift up all those you can lift up
And carry all those that you can carry
And love all those that you can
And pray for all those that you can pray for
That time will work to your advantage
Which works to the advantage of God
Because He holds time in the palm of his hands
And He is the only one that will let you know
That because you subdued your free will
And submitted yourself to His will

That you are chosen to sit on the council
That will pass judgment upon angels

CYPHA FOR JESUS

You are my source of energy and inspiration
When my world collapses into a chasm of desperation
Nobody fathoms what I'm feeling
Forcing me to play that nasty hand they've been dealing me
Constantly deceived and manipulated
I was consumed by my own hatred
Always agitated
But You, You are my guide
As I make my way through the treachery and wilderness
No longer must I hide
'Cause I got You by my side
Through the thick and thin
You help me to fulfill my earthly mission
Providing that extra input that I need to make the right decisions
So, there's no need to dust off the shovels
Cause nobody has to die, as I progress to the next levels
Using my third eye's intuition
I make a change in the way I live
I change how I talk
I stand strong as I walk
Through this wicked world we live in nowadays
I'm not caught up in the glitz or glamor or blunted haze
The way I was back then
I look back and wonder
How did I survive that walking slumber?
If not for the Lord
I would still be asleep
My character would still be weak
My thoughts would not be nearly as deep
I look at the next generation that's up and coming
Some are seeking the wisdom, while some are fools just stumbling
Through the same moments of discombobulated directions
Slipping into darkness because they don't know who to seek for protection
He, who manifested in the flesh, from the Spirit
If you're working for the enemy, you might not want to hear it
That name, which has authority, power, and glory
Jesus Christ, not the superstar
But the Son, who did that which none could do again
Paid for you, you, you, you, and me, my friend
There when you call, and even when you don't
Leave your side, He said that He won't

Yet, we need to see the footsteps in the sand
The path that was left by the Spirit Man
That led the way, and still leads
Every man needeth faith the size of a simple mustard seed
But sometimes we can't see
We're blinded because we move through life selfishly
Thinking it's all about us
Nah! It's not about us
It's about Jesus
What He did in the past
Nothing we do, would ever outlast
Seek the Son if you seek peace, and want to be free
He'll do it for you, like He's done it for me

[A meditation on **Hebrews 12:2** *Looking unto Jesus, the Author and Finisher of our faith, who for the joy that was set before Him endured the cross, despising the shame, and is set down at the right hand of the throne of God.*]

I WILL NOT GIVE UP

When the world was being created, the Lord had a dream
On this dream, He did not give up
When the Lord finished creating all manner of creatures to occupy the earth
He did not give up
When the Lord finished creating all manner of creatures to occupy the earth
He did not give up
When He decided that all those things were good
He decided that they were not enough
So, God sat down, picked up a handful of clay and He began to design the most intricate object
He created man
He made man in His own image, with the idea that if man looks like Me
Man should understand his relation to Me and therefore do as I tell him to do
And He looked at this man, whom He named Adam; the Appointed Disciple
Anointed Man, and said to Himself, this is good
He told man to name all of the creatures before him
He wanted to see just how intelligent His creation was
And He saw the power of man's mind, and He thought, this is good
He watched man and noticed that man was somber because he did not have what every other one of God's creations had, a partner, a balance
God thought to Himself, this is not good
So, God caused man to fall asleep; He took a rib from His unique creation
He took that rib and fashioned a masterpiece
He looked at this work of art and spoke
"This one, I will call Wo-man, because this one was created from the womb of man"
HE saw HIS work, and HE named her Eve
She was to be to Adam, a physical representation of God's love
He presented Eve to Adam and thus began the world
Now Adam and Even moved through the world
God looked upon them with favor
God walked with Adam every morning

God spoke to Adam every day
Why do we not speak to Him every day?
Let's examine this
Adam fell short of the Word that he received directly from the mouth of God
And we wonder why we cannot live up to the Word of God today
However, I pose the question
Should we not strive to live by the Word even when we disagree?
Does not the Lord God know more about our futures than we could ever imagine?
The Word says that God cannot be tempted by evil
He also says that He will not tempt us with evil
He would not force us to do something that is against His Word
I ask you to do this
When you are faced with a decision, do you think, "What would God want me to do?"
Or do you lean unto your own understanding?
The Word of the Lord is the Truth, and the Way
The Word became physical at one point in the world's history because God did not give up
We always hear things like "let it go"!
Let it go means let go of the sinful part of what we are dealing with
Whether it is anger
Whether it is frustration
Whether it is fear
Whether it is guilt
If you are following in the Word of God
If you are believing in the Word of God
When you have feelings that you know you should not have
Do what God says do, lay those burdens on HIM
He did not say that you would not face these problems
HE said that you should not give up
Job didn't give up
After the loss of his children
Job did not give up
After he lost his herds
Job did not give up
After he lost all that God had blessed him with
He never said it was God that was doing this to him
What he said was

11

If I have done something to offend you, Lord God
Let me know what it was
He said, I will stand for the Lord no matter what
Till there be no more breath in my body
When the man was riding on his donkey
And the donkey stopped because of the angel standing in its path
Ready to strike down his rider
That man, Balaam, beat that donkey
Can you imagine this?
Beating the donkey until it didn't even want to stand anymore
That donkey could have said
"You know what? You hit me one more time and I'm going to move so that the angel of the Lord can slay you and relieve me of the burden of you"
But the donkey loved his master enough to save his life
Jonah didn't go where he was supposed to go; so, God went and brought him where HE wanted Jonah to be
The Word speaks of Jesus and the temptation of Jesus, by the enemy
One crucial point, I believe we all miss
When Jesus was being tempted
The Word says,
Satan "TOOK" Jesus from place to place
It does not say that Jesus <u>followed</u> Satan
That means that Satan can move you, if God gives him leave to do so
Don't misunderstand me; Satan has to ask for permission to do this
But God can grant him this power
When he has been given permission Satan can do a lot
However, when God grants him permission to use things against you
You must stand on the promises
Which are written in the Word
Which were represented when the WORD
Put on flesh and lived and lived as we lived for 33 years
That same Word was sacrificed to save us all
Because even though we are not worthy
Even though we do not deserve it
Even though we can never get close enough to truly be considered righteous in God's eyes
He loved us; He cared for us
He made the sacrifice, He made a way
He wants us all to be with HIM, in the end

He wants us to come back
He wants us to share in His glory
And for this
He; God; The Father
The Son; Jesus Christ
The Comforter
The Holy Spirit
Did not give up on us
Therefore, I must say
That no matter what comes
No matter what I may go through
I will stand on His Word
I will stand on His Promises
I will stand for Him and
I will not give up!

Inspired by **Ecclesiastes 9:11** (KJV) [*I returned, and saw under the sun, that the race is not to the swift, nor the battle to the strong, neither yet bread to the wise, nor yet riches to men of understanding, nor yet favour to men of skill; but time and chance happeneth to them all.*]

I HAVE YOUR BEST INTEREST AT HEART
(A conversation from God's perspective)

Hello, I have your best interest at heart
I am your neighbor
I see all that you have and how you say, my Father gave it to you
Yeah Right!
I see how you drink alcohol and smoke pot on your back porch
When you think no one is aware
I see how you make sure that you have the best clothing and the expensive car
But you drove by me when my car was stopped on the side of the road
I have your best interest at heart
I am your boss
If you work for me, I have a reward for you
I allow you to add increase to all that you have
Show me that you are worth my investment and I will invest more into you
But I hear you complain about what I do not do for you
You give me eight hours of work; I give you eight hours of pay
Am I not holding up my end of the bargain?
Why do you speak ill of me?
I see you; I hear you
You speak against me, but I still have your best interest at heart
I am your friend
When you needed someone to talk to you called me
Did I not answer?
When you struggled and needed a hand
Did I not freely give unto you and ask for nothing in return?
Then why, when I called on you, did you not answer?
When I needed you to give some of your overflow to someone in need
Why didn't you?
When I tried to talk to you, why did you not listen?
I have always had your best interest at heart
I am your lover,
I gave myself unto you freely
I love you now, even though you show me no love
I submitted to you and gave you my all
Yet you abused me, you led me astray
You knew that you were unsure before we came together
But instead of loving me enough to think of me first, you only thought of yourself
You don't listen, you hardened your mind
You hardened your heart
You've covered your ears so that you cannot hear me

14

You accept without question everything else but what I wrote down for you
As a concrete reminder of what you mean to Me
I have never left you; I even protect you when you reject me
You have the nerve to wonder
To question
If I have your best interest at heart
When God made the world, He moved but we didn't exist so we couldn't see
When God made man, HE moved
After God made Adam, He gave him an assignment,
Name all creatures big and small
God saw when Adam realized he had no mate
God saw this need, this desire, and God moved
When Adam disobeyed God's instruction
God moved, when the children of Israel cried out for deliverance,
God moved, when the children of Israel lived in the wilderness with no food
God moved, when Pharaoh pursued the children of Israel
God moved, when the children of Israel were led to their freedom by God's appointed and they disobeyed God
God moved when we wanted to know if our prayers meant anything to God
HE told us that the prayers of the righteous avails much
This means that God does move, even today
The problem is, when HE moves, are we qualified enough
To know that it is God's movement
Do we understand the WORD when God moved?
Do we recognize His guidance when we are going through?
Do we recognize God's direction when we are forced into a situation we disagree with?
Do we think about what Jesus would do when HE gave HIS Word and are faced with insurmountable odds?

[The inspiration for this: What God wants for you will exceed what you want for yourself, per **John 10:10** (KJV) *The thief cometh not, but for to steal, and to kill, and to destroy: I am come that they might have life, and that they might have it more abundantly.*]

ISN'T IT FUNNY?

Isn't it funny how we can listen to the Word of God, but not hear the message?
Isn't it funny how we believe that God should work for us,
Even though we perform no work for Him.
Isn't it funny how we hear when we want to hear?
Isn't it funny how we can believe in the blessings but not in the entire Word?
Or better yet
Isn't it funny how we can believe in the parts of the Word that we agree with and discard the rest?
Isn't it funny how we can study the Word. . .?
We can speak it, we can quote it
We say that we are instruments for the Lord's work
Yet, when we are faced with something that doesn't line up with what the Word says
We believe it, before we believe the Word?
It's funny,
When we are supposed to be Believers
Who have faith in Jesus,
Faith in the Word of God
But we refuse to follow that Word!
Isn't that a contradiction?
Isn't it funny how we can understand that God made man with family in mind; but,
We believe that we do not need our family.
You see, Satan was created by God also,
He rebelled against the family and, he continues to do so
Isn't it funny how we don't believe that withdrawing from family is an action from the enemy?
Isn't it funny how we believe that witchcraft and sorcery are evil?
Yet, when we call ourselves talking to God,
We have to have certain things around us because we believe those objects have some property that is going to give us more favor with God.
Isn't it funny?
When Jesus spoke, He spoke in parables
Which are defined as simple stories that illustrate a moral or religious lesson
Yet witchcraft uses objects as symbols, or something that represents
Something else by association, resemblance, or convention, especially a material object used to represent something invisible

However, it would seem that it is more important to believe in the symbols than in the parables themselves
Isn't it funny? We can believe in dreams, visions and prophecies that can be changed with the winds over the promises written in the Word that does not change
Isn't it funny? How we are supposed to be Believers, who live by a different set of rules
Yet, when we disagree with those guidelines, we justify what we do by saying that the problem is with the interpretation
As Christians we are an interesting breed
We believe in God, but we don't want to listen to His directions
We believe in the Word, but only in certain parts
We believe that when we sin,
Even if we know at the time that we're committing sin
We believe that God is going to simply forgive us because HIS Son paid the price for us
But I pose a question, isn't it funny that we say we want to get closer to HIM
Yet we don't want to truly understand His last message
Love one another, for Love covers a multitude of sins
Isn't it funny how we want to play with God?
Like He's one of our homies?
Isn't it funny how we don't like when people use our words against us?
Yet, we use God's words against Him?
Isn't it funny how we think that because we simply believe, but aren't willing to work at changing ourselves, that we are going to be saved?
God will show you what you need to work on
Sometimes, He will speak directly to you
Sometimes, He will allow you to experience the same circumstances over and over again until you learn the lesson
Other times, He will use someone else to show you
But isn't it funny, how when He doesn't speak directly to you,
That you don't receive it unless it is from someone you have trust in
Actually, there are times that you only receive the message from someone outside of your circle of trust.
Isn't it funny how God has no respect for any person?
But we believe that He should do it the way that we want Him to otherwise we don't listen!
Now, isn't that funny?

[Inspired by meditation on **Psalm 78:22**: *Because they believed not in God, and trusted not in his salvation*]

WHICH WAY DO I GO?

As I walk along the pathway
I come to a fork in the road and I wonder, which way?
One way looks clean yet well used
One way looks like it hasn't been used for a while
I chose this path with a smile
You may wonder why
If you listen it will become clear
If you listen with your heart
You'll understand what you hear
The well-traveled path looked the same as the one that led me to this point
Same trees, same breeze, same dusky sky
This was all a routine; I needed something new to try
The path less traveled was different
Just a tad overgrown
It was the type of path that one must travel alone
It didn't look easy
Matter of fact, it looked like it would be a lot of work
But if you receive without struggle, do you understand the worth?
Sometimes there will be storms, sometimes there will be floods
But It's worth it. Believing in the strength of the blood
The other pathway was easy, I could see far from where I stood
Too easy if I took it, then regret it I would
I could see money in piles, cars and big houses
Smiling women in tight skirts, and low-cut blouses
I could see the other brothers, way down that path
But there was something in their eyes that showed it would not last
Which way do I go? I made up my mind
To take the journey with the path that I would have to find
The one that made me work, struggle and strive
The one that challenged my faith, and why I believe I'm alive
Which way do I go? It's the simplest choice
I choose the path from which comes my Savior's voice
The way that I go for me, is the way that is true

I hope the direction you choose is the path less traveled, which will take you
To the Savior too!

[Thoughts based on meditation regarding **Psalm 119:105:** *Your word is a lamp for my feet, a light on my path* and **Proverbs 3:5-6**: *Trust in the Lord with all thine heart; and lean not unto thine own understanding. In all thy ways acknowledge him, and he shall direct thy paths.*]

RED POEM

Red has been explained as the color of extreme emotion
Red is the color of roses given in love
Red is the box of candies
Red is usually used as an expression of passion
But the best expression of the color of Red
Was in the Blood of Christ
The Blood that was given to pay the price
The price that was paid to save our lives
The Blood that washed away all sin
The Living Blood that has no end
The Blood that was spilled during HIS persecution
Christ did not try to beg his way out of execution
The Son of God did not barter or trade
He knew the purpose for which He was made
I wonder what He thought during that time
Saving our souls was His purpose, and His crime
Do we have what it takes to live up to the task
Live according to His ways was all that He asked
We suffer for a while and blame the Father
He suffered for us as if it was no bother
You complain when money is tight, and bills are due
He complained not once as the nails were forced through
How we lived yesterday we must change
How we live today, we must arrange
How we live tomorrow, we must choose
The Blood was spilled so that we cannot lose
Are you able to give?
Your love, your compassion, your energy, your knowledge, your gifts
As long as you give of yourself
On behalf of the Lord
In the name of Christ
You will be a true example of one with Christ in your life

[Inspired by **John 3:16:** *For God so loved the world, that he gave his only begotten Son, that whosoever believeth on him should not perish, but have eternal life.*]

THIS CHRISTMAS
An Ode to Christ

During this Christmas season,
I'm forced to think
of how Christ the Savior
pulled me back from the brink
I was walking about in a shadowy mist
Dead on my feet, yet I didn't know this
All my efforts were failing, I continued to try, shot down time and time again; I didn't know why. Then I heard a voice off down the way, and I could see a light that made the night like day. As I got closer, I saw His outstretched hands, patiently waiting to embrace this torn and tattered man. I was hesitant at first
because I wasn't sure
But He let me know that His love was pure
The closer I got, I had to cover my eyes
The light was so blinding much to my surprise
He asked me did I love Him, and did I believe?
At first, I wondered, was there something up HIS sleeve?
He laughed until tears came from His eyes
He said do you understand why I gave up my life?
I told him, because I'd never make the measure
So blemished am I, that His Father would not see me as treasure
He smiled again and embraced me with a warmth I struggle to describe
As the essence of Love, for which He gave up His life
He told me you will do things for My kingdom as long as you stay
Strong in your faith, repentance, and continue to pray
I smiled and tears streamed down my face
I understood that He'd already won the race
I didn't deserve it, this even I knew
He said, you do deserve it, simply because I love you
So, this Christmas,
If you are missing something, or someone in your life
Ask for that emptiness to be filled by none other than Christ

[Written 12/07/2003: Inspired by the understanding of what the season of Christmas really represents. **Ephesians 2:8-9 (NKJV)** *For by grace you have been saved through faith, and that not of yourselves; it is the gift of God, not of works, lest anyone should boast.*]

WHAT DO YOU BELIEVE IN?

Do you believe in the Father, The Son, and The Holy Ghost?
To answer this question
You must first be honest with yourself
1 Corinthians 3:18 tells us *"Let no man deceive himself. If any man among you seemeth to be wise in this world, let him become a fool, that he may be wise."*
See, many of us deceive ourselves
We say that we are Christians
We say that we believe in the death, burial and resurrection of Christ
We say that we believe that God can supply all our needs
But what do we really believe in?
We believe in what is tangible
What we can hold in our hands
We believe in the promises of the Bible
While we are reading it!
While it is in our hands because it is the tangible expression of the Word of God
However,
When it is out of sight, and out of reach
We seem to forget what the Word tells us
We forget that God said, if He feeds and clothes the birds
Surely, we are more precious than they
We believe that God made the heavens and the Earth
Yet sometimes we don't believe that He is still present
I ask you a question
Where would you be?
Right this moment, if God, truly left you
You would cease to exist
Not just die
You would cease
God holds your very molecules and atoms together
Even when you are not heeding what He wants you to do
You see we are busy believing that we know what is right
We believe that we can tell who is serving the Lord by our own sight
We believe that we have the right to deny someone else's calling
What do we really believe in?
For Jesus said let him who is greatest amongst you
Be the least and him who is least be the greatest
For Jesus served
Though he was, and is, and will be the greatest that will ever exist
We believe in titles
We believe in wealth
We believe in what we can manipulate to make us seem better than we are

Jesus already made it possible for us to be so much more than we are capable of being by ourselves
What is a minister?
A minister is one who is authorized to perform religious functions in a Christian church
Who gives the authorization?
He, who has all the power
It is not the power of the man before you
It is the power of the oath, and who you are making the oath to
What do you believe in?
Do you believe in the power of the Word?
If, in the beginning; there was only God
The Word of God caused everything to come into existence
If you cannot trust in His Word,
In whose words can you believe?
Our problem
We are more worried about proving what has been changed than we are about getting the point
The point is not to belittle one another
That's not the way that God intended us to be
We shouldn't be at war with each other over the meaning of the Word
Not saying that we should not have a thirst
A thirst for as much of the Word, in its truest form as we can get
But the purpose of the Word is not to cause chaos
The purpose of the Word is not to cause confusion
The only one that should be confused by the Word of God
Should be the enemy and those who are his allies
1 Corinthians 14:33 says *"For God is not the author of confusion, but of peace, as in all churches of the saints."*
When we are envious of each other
When we are jealous of each other
When we are trying to get what others have because we want it
There, then, will be confusion
James 3:16 states *"For where envy and strife is, there is confusion and every evil work"*
We are so caught up in what we do not have
We do not have the latest Cadillac Escalade or Lexus
We do not have a Rolex
We do not have what multi-millionaires have
We do not have the looks of Will Smith or Denzel Washington
Halle Berry or Angela Bassett
We do not have the talent of Luther or Whitney
We do not have the physique of those men and women that we see
On Tell Lie Vision

We are not as smart as Einstein or Dubois
Man, that is a lot of "***nots***" to have in your life
But you see, a knot is what it is because of the twisting
When we see what others have, that we do not
There comes the twisting
We twist the road that we must travel
We twist the reason that we do not have what they have
We twist, at some point in time, what we believe in
We believe that we do not have the intelligence
Because God did not bless us with it
Here's a twist
When God created man, He tasked man to name all the animals
Genesis 2:19 "*And out of the ground the LORD God formed every beast of the field, and every fowl of the air; and brought them unto Adam to see what he would call them: and whatsoever Adam called every living creature, that was the name thereof*"
When God gave Adam this task, the Word does not say that God led man in what He wanted everything to be called
This lets us know that our intelligence is only limited by ourselves
Adam did not have a book to read the names of the animals from, nor to record them in
He did not have a television to show him the picture to go with the name
He did what God asked using one of the most powerful items that God gave us: The Mind
What do you believe in?
Do you believe in God?
Do you believe in the Son, The Savior, Jesus Christ?
Do you believe that through Him, all things are possible?
Do you understand?
God will give talents to whom He decides to give talents to
God will pour out gifts on whomever He chooses to
Do you understand that if you have a gift or a talent, but you are not using it to the best of your ability, this does not demonstrate a belief in God?
Do you understand that sitting on your gift or talent is what may be hindering you?
What do you believe in?
If you believe in God
His Word, that became flesh
Lived as a man, died as a perfect man
Who paid for you and me?
You know, the beginning and the end
The only way for you and me to receive eternal life
Then what you believe in is rooted in righteousness
However, if you believe that one gift

Whether it be speaking in tongues
Or singing, writing, teaching
Preaching, visions
Prophecy, casting out spirits
Has any actual bearing on your eternal soul
You may have missed the mark
For worthy is He that seeketh the Lord in all that he doeth
For seeking the Lord first
Causes you to first be humble
To then give your will to His will
To then do what He wants you to do
To think of Him
The Father
The Son
And the Holy Ghost
Then and only then will you be
Showing what you believe in.
Written 02/10/2004

GOD'S MAN

What does it mean to be God's Man?
The concept in itself seems to be redundant
The important word of this thought is, Good
The root of good is God
For all that is good is of God
And if you are rooted in God, then in essence, you should be good
But you have a problem
We were born in sin
Which means; we are bad
This means it is easier for us to do the devil's handiwork than it is to do God's
Let's think about this for a minute
The word devil means
Deception, envy, vanity, ignorance, lies
When you offer someone deception instead of reality
This is not good
When you are envious of someone
This too is not good
When you are constantly focused on yourself
Focused on what you've achieved
This is vanity
This is wrong
When you can't uplift someone else during your struggle
You are suffering from ignorance
This is wrong
When it is more important for you to lie to someone
When you go through great lengths not to tell them the truth
This is a lie
This too is wrong
If you have any desire to be a true light for the world
You must first seek the goodness of God in all that you do
How do you seek Him?
You must first go through HIS Son, Jesus Christ
You see Christ knew how easy it would have been
To not do HIS Father's work
But HE chose the harder road
The Bible tells us that the road of righteousness is narrow
And hard
Yet the road to damnation is wide
And easy, for many will travel its pathway
You see we have a problem distinguishing the good that is of God
From the good that we feel we are able to accomplish

Let me explain
Psalm 50:6 reads, *and the heavens shall declare his righteousness: for God judge himself*
What does this mean?
This means that just because we think it's right does not mean it is
For only God can judge what you do to be righteous
How can you find out if what you are doing is of God?
Well, let us look
From the, I want to be God's man, point of view
Psalm 71:24 *My tongue also shall talk of thy righteousness all the day long: For they are confounded, for they are brought unto shame, that seek my hurt*
In your times of struggle
Do you say Oh, God; I've been praying to you about this for a long time, long time
Why has this not changed?
This is not a tongue speaking of righteousness
For God said He hears the prayers of the righteous
Sometimes, we hinder our own prayers because of repetition
We keep asking God about the same things over and over again
Then we sit in confusion because we don't see anything changing with a timeframe that we would like something to happen
Well. . .
Didn't God say, "your thoughts are not my thoughts"?
Didn't God say, "your ways are not my ways"?
And let me ask you this
When you are on your job
And your boss calls you every fifteen seconds
To ask you to do the same thing
How much have you accomplished of the duty assigned to you within the ten minutes between calls?
If you have been interrupted 40 times
That's once every fifteen seconds
You haven't accomplished anything
And if you have, you are better than many of us
Because your train of thought keeps getting interrupted and even you are being told the same thing over and over
You can't do anything because the time it takes for you to hang up your phone
Read what may be on your monitor, which may be an email from your boss about the same thing he or she just called you about
Or the project that you are working on; and where you were before you got interrupted
You get interrupted again
You can't get anything accomplished
Well, we know that GOD does not get distracted like we do

27

However, if you believe in Jesus Christ
Then when you pray for something
You need only pray once, or for a certain period of time
Then let it go
For Christ said to cast your burdens on me
That means, if you fasted and prayed for that time period
You are required to let it go and Let God
Pray on it, then move on to the next issue, perhaps for somebody else this time
Because if your focus is only on you
You might not get what you need from God
You see, God tells us, "Love thy enemies"
That means even though they may speak evil of you
They may do evil to you
They may plot to harm you
You are still supposed to love them
You are still supposed to lift them up to HIM in prayer
You are still supposed to deal with them as if they've done you no harm
Because when Jesus was spit upon
He could have put down His cross
Raised His fists
And beat the mess out of His oppressors like He did the merchants when they were disrespecting His Father's House
But He did not do this
Mind you
He had and still has all the power
But He suffered through to save us
He spoke to His Father and said forgive them for they know not what they do
You see, the truth is
Nothing of worth
Can be had without struggle
The old cliché
Nothing from nothing leaves nothing
Is another way of saying
You see, if you are trying to be God's Man
Then you will do what He says, in His Word
Yes, you will stumble; Yes, you will fall
Yes, you will suffer
Sometimes by the hand of others
Sometimes by your own
If someone has caused you pain
Instead of holding onto it
Cast it all on Jesus and move on
Husbands, if you don't love your wives as you love yourselves
If you don't treat them with respect as you would yourself

If you don't pray for her
You will hinder your prayers for yourself
If you don't pray with her
Your prayers may not be answered
Wives, if you don't respect the authority of the man you chose to accept as your husband
For God said the choice to marry is yours
The Word of God tells us that for those of us who do marry; there will be oppression in the flesh
You may wonder what this means.
What you used to do; you may not be able to do anymore, because now this affects more than just you
Your spirituality is connected to the man that you chose to accept as the leader of your household
How is this?
If he is God's man
He is to pray with you
Before he is able to lay with you
He should love you, not put himself above you
He is to feed you with the Word of God
Just as he feeds himself from the Bible
He is supposed to consult the Word when he is right and when he is wrong
He is to be strong enough in his faith to understand that there are going to be times when his decision may be wrong; but,
He has to be able to make the decisions that God said he is to make
No ladies, I know that this is entitled "God's Man"
But the word "man," in this case, speaks of the race of mankind
Not just the male gender
Because women have always achieved great things
They have their own money, they have their own jobs
Businesses, transportation, ministries even
But here's the kicker
If you have all these things
Yet you have no one to share them with
And your soul is heavy because of the desire to have a partner
Is your desire to have a partner wrong? No!
The issue though, is that when they come along the road
And you let them into your life, do you control them? No!
Do they control you? No!
You are supposed to complement one another
Many get confused by what this really means
You should be equally yoked
This phrase does not mean
You should have the same amount of money

It does not mean
You should have the exact same ideas
It does not mean
That your ministries are going to be the same
But wait
Your ministries
Maybe this is the issue
If the ministries indeed are your own
This is the problem
For the servitude to God's people
Does not belong to men or women
It belongs to God
But if your frame of mind is that the ministry belongs to you
Then you are in fact not God's Man
Because He has given you everything to do a job for Him
And as with any job
There are guidelines
You can't take care of His house
Without taking care of yours
Your house is the first component of the ministry He has chosen for you
Proverbs 11:6 *The righteousness of the upright shall deliver them: but transgressors shall be taken in their own naughtiness*
When you do what God wants you to do
Sometimes it will be tough on you
It's tough because He wants to test you
He wants to see if you are truly a Believer in Him
He wants to know what is truly in your heart
As long as it is going well, you will do His work
But when you begin to struggle, do you
Seek His guidance?
Or do you lean to your own understanding?
Do you read the Word which plainly tells you there will be oppression in the flesh?
Do you take that to mean only for the sinner?
Well, you are a sinner
Yes, you may have been saved by grace
But this does not eliminate the fact that you are a sinner
This only allows you to be represented by Christ
Because of your faith in Him
Does knowing this give you a license to play with the word of the Lord?
NO!
What do I mean by playing?
When you ask God what to do
When the answer in the Word tells you what to do

Do you say nope!
I'm not going to follow what the word says
I'm going to do what I believe needs to be done
But the Word plainly tells you most of the time
But we don't believe that the Word is actually meant for us in our situation
But this goes back to what do you believe in?
You cannot dissect the Word of God into only what you want to accept
When you accept Christ into your life
You have to understand that the instructions are given for you to follow
If you don't follow them
The road may seem easier
It may even seem fun
You may even prosper
For a while
But what happens when the race is over
And you haven't crossed the finish line?
A lot of us won't make it to the finish line because we are not representing the Lord
We say we are, but we are not
When we say that we believe in God
But this section of the Word does not pertain to us
We are not God's men
When we say that we believe in God
But for some reason, we just can't forgive and move on because
We are still hurting
We are not being God's men
When we say that we understand that we are going to suffer sometimes
But when the suffering comes, we run from the situation
We are not being God's men
Well, you may be wondering how to become God's man
When you follow the rules
Through the pain
Through the suffering
Through the weights of the world
Through the plots against you by the enemy
God tells us in
Matthew 5:44 "*But I tell you, Love your enemies, bless those who curse you, do good to those who hate you, and pray for those who spitefully use you and persecute you.*"
You see it is so much easier to love those who love you
It's easy to give love when you are getting love
It's easier to excel in the world of men, when men encourage you
It's easier also to lose sight of what the Word says to you
The Lord tells us

The Lord warns us
I too have been caught looking in the other direction
I too have been caught sleeping on the job
Matthew 24:43 tells us, *"But know this, that if the goodman of the house had known in what watch the thief would come, he would have watched, and would not have suffered his house to be broken up."*
This does not mean that we are going to see everything before it happens
However, God does see it all, He knows it all
He gives you glimpses of what the road ahead will be if you continue doing
What you are doing
But God's man must be steadfast in the Word of God
He must always refer to the Word for his inspiration
He must always refer to the Word for his direction
He must always refer to the Word for his dedication
For man shall always fall short
Matthew 24:4 prepares us for the nature of man as it tells us, *"And Jesus answered and said unto them, Take heed that no man deceive you"*
This is not to say that, should you be deceived; that you are not God's man
This means that just as Christ, God's son, was lied on, lied about, set up, convicted and crucified
Simply because of the misshaped, warped, twisted, contorted minds of fleshly men
Also, too, will be the good man; God's man

[Thinking about what it takes to be God's man based on **John 6:45:** *It is written in the prophets, And they shall be all taught of God. Every man therefore that hath heard, and hath learned of the Father, cometh unto me.* Also, **Proverbs 3:5-6:** *Trust in the Lord with all your heart, And lean not on your own understanding; In all your ways acknowledge Him, And He shall direct your paths.*]

SO YOU CALL YOURSELF A CHRISTIAN

Greetings, today is the day that you define who, and what you are
Today is the day that we re-examine what our purpose is
Today is the day that we must clarify our focus
Most of us are walking around spiritually blind
The funny thing is that we don't even realize that we are.
Our faith has been beat down
Our faith has been manipulated
Into this little switch that we click on when we are in the church
And we click it off as soon as we walk out of the door
And you call yourself a Christian
The problem is that our blindness comes from dealing with the things that we see
We are also deaf because of all the things that we've heard
We are this way because of each other
Let me clarify, we are this way because of other Believers
You see, Believers are supposed to live by a different set of rules
The rules or guidelines that are grounded in the Bible
Our problem is this:
When we walk through this world, we don't realize how easy it is to
Get caught up in what we want and not what God wants for us
Mark 8:33 *But when He had turned around and looked at His disciples, He rebuked Peter, saying, "Get behind Me, Satan! For you are not mindful of the things of God, but the things of men."*
You see, Peter was caught up by Satan
Peter was a great disciple of Christ
But even he was fooled from time to time by Satan
What makes you think that you can't be?
What makes you think that you can't be?
What makes you think that you can see it coming?
What makes you think that you are so holier-than-thou that you are above rebuking?
And you call yourself a Christian
For while Job was going through even his friends fell into the simple traps of the enemy
But, Job being the righteous man, recognized this was happening and he addressed it
Job 36:10 tells us, *"He openeth also their ear to discipline, and commandeth that they return from iniquity."*
You see, from the beginning, the enemy was lurking about trying to destroy those created in God's image
The enemy is mad at every human being! He is really ticked off

He has been for a long time, and he is going to come after you
And he will get you if you are not prepared
Matter of fact, he will get you because you think that you prepared for everything that he can throw at you. This is possible but not with that frame of mind
You see, the wickedness was brought about by the twisting that the enemy did within the Garden of Eden
This place that man was given (notice I said given)
Not that man purchased or earned it
This alone shows us how good God is
But I digress, after the enemy tempted man's mate
She, in turn, began to do the enemy's will
She tempted her husband
To eat the fruit from the tree of the knowledge of good and evil
But let me remind you that there were two trees in the garden that man was not to partake
   1. The tree of the knowledge of good and evil
   2. The tree of Life
Here is the issue that I find interesting about this particular temptation
Man had a chance, a chance to choose eternal life
All he had to do, was go to the other tree first
Do you have a clue as to where I am going?
Well, I'll help you in just a second
We know that the enemy tempted Eve
She, being corrupted, but not the head, lived in misery
And you've heard of the old saying that misery loves company
You also must understand that if a poisonous snake bites you on your foot
And you don't receive the antidote within a certain amount of time
That poison will travel throughout the body and cause the nerves within your body to stop responding to the control of the mind. Now, the mind's whole purpose is to control the body. If it cannot control the body, then it has no purpose and therefore, it shuts down over time because it has no control, and you die. That's the way it works in the flesh
But aren't you glad that God is not of the flesh?
I know that I am
Whew! But let me get back on track.
You see, once man ate from the tree of the knowledge of good and evil
The alarm went off on God's pager
Alerting Him, the Trinity
The Bible tells us in **Genesis 3:22** (KJV) *"And the LORD God said, Behold, the man is become as one of us, to know good and evil: and now, lest he put forth his hand, and take also of the tree of life, and eat, and live forever"*
Now I don't know if you recall what I said earlier about man having a chance to receive eternal life from the beginning but here it is

You see knowledge is given by the Father to those who serve Him, and those who ask
Adam went for long walks with God every day
Yet while walking in all that glory
He never thought to ask God about living forever
Even after his instructions told him that if you should eat from the tree of knowledge
That he would surely die
You may wonder why this never entered his mind
If you don't, you should
You see, even then the Word of God gives you knowledge
But if you are not paying attention to the Word of God
You might miss it; you might say that it's confusing
For the Lord said that He is not the author of confusion
But if you look toward the hills from which cometh your help
You will see that tree of life that was referred to in **Genesis 3:22**
Was the physical, tangible embodiment of Christ
You may not accept this but here are the clues
You see when Christ was placed within the womb of Mary
She was informed of what He was going to do
As Christ grew up, ministered, healed, expelled demons and, brought some people back from the dead, God had a plan
When Christ was beaten and whipped and tortured
What did they give him to carry?
A crucifix!
A crucifix made of wood
Wood = the wood of a tree
This is significant because
The earthly father of Christ was a carpenter; therefore, so was the Savior
What does a carpenter do? He takes the tree
Which, when growing on its own seems to be very chaotic
And he shapes and molds it into something that is beautiful to look at
But most importantly, he makes it useful
Now I'm not saying if you didn't come to this conclusion that you are not a Christian
I'm not saying that you are not full of faith
I'm just saying that you can always go deeper into the Word of God
You may need to ask for more wisdom, knowledge and understanding
You need to realize that everything that happens to you has a purpose
You see, the enemy's purpose is to break you
To destroy you
To kill you
First in your mind; next in your body; then you soul
But the LORD takes the plan of the enemy and uses it for good

As the enemy tries to break down your mind, getting you to idolize things of this world
Money, cars, clothes, property, people
God wants to fortify your mind by feeding your mind with His Word
Where the enemy may trick you into doing something that will taint the temple that
The LORD hath given to you
The LORD will take that and use it to build your resolve to do His will even more
He will rid your body of whatever it may be, to give you a testimony about His goodness
And when the enemy attacks you spiritually
You may pray
You may cry out unto the Lord
But you have no strength in these times
But the Lord has all the strength that you need
For through your weakness, you will see His strength
He will protect you
Through it all
As Believers, we sometimes stumble and fall
And sometimes we lay down
I get so tired of people using the phrase
"If it is God's will," as a cop out
God's will is not something that we cannot comprehend.
You call yourself a Christian
Turn to His Word if you want to know what God's will is
Turn to His Word if you want to know why you are struggling
Turn to His Word if you want to know how to get your increase
Turn to His Word if you no longer want to live in fear
Turn to His Word if you want to proclaim Him as your Lord and Savior, and walk in boldness,
In His name, turn to His Word
The days of miracles are still here
But we misunderstand what a miracle is
Today the miracle is finding a Believer who not only knows the Word of God
But also, they are truly trying to live by it
It is a miracle to find a church home without hypocrites within it
It is a miracle to find people who are willing to serve the Lord
Without having their hands out
It is a miracle
If your mind is receiving this
That God loved us, so much that He gave His only begotten Son to save us all
I ask you, I beg of you
Please, my brothers and sisters in Christ

Study the Word
Think the Word
See it with your mind and heart
And ultimately
Live by it
For then, and only then, will you truly be
A disciple worthy of being called a Christian

[Ruminations on **John 14:15:** "If you love me, keep my commands."]

HAVE YOU LOST YOUR MIND?

Today, is a crucial moment in the history of your walk with Christ
Today you will either arrive at a moment of brilliant clarity or you will spend many more
Years stumbling and bumbling around like an infant in a walker
Today's question is very important:
Have you lost your mind?
The reason for this question is the number of complications that you may experience in you have
In fact, lost your marbles
You see, we as human beings are always trying to understand exactly what God has in store for us
In other words, we want to know the mind of God
The Bible tells us that people were concerned about what was going on in God's mind
Leviticus 24:12 *Then they put him in custody, that the mind of the LORD might be shown to them.*
Unfortunately for the young man that was put inward: the Lord's mind was on vengeance and he was stoned to death by the inhabitants of his camp
But you see, we spend so much time focused on the wrong things
We focus on what God may be thinking
Instead of focusing on what His Word tells us that we should be doing
For instance: If someone offered you money to speak of foul and sinful things
What would you do?
Numbers 24:13: *If Balak were to give me his house full of silver and gold, I could not go beyond the word of the LORD, to do good or bad of my own will. What the LORD says, that I must speak'?*
You see, nothing, and I repeat nothing, should take precedence over the will of the Lord
But you see, this is where the sinful flesh messes us up
You see we are all sinful by nature
Romans 3:10: *There is none righteous, No, Not one.*
But you see, we, as human beings
Those of us who claim Christ as our Savior
Those of us who talk the talk
Act as though we are walking the walk
You see, we have lost our minds
We use this statement as a crutch
As we find numerous scriptural crutches
We stand upon these scriptures when we mess up
We say, "See? Even the Bible says that we mess up."
I ask you though, was it not Paul, who said

1 Timothy 1:12-13: *"And I thank Christ Jesus our Lord, who hath enabled me, for that he counted me faithful, putting me into the ministry, who was before a blasphemer, and a persecutor, and injurious: but I obtained mercy, because I did it ignorantly in unbelief"*
This is a very powerful and cutting scripture
For Paul tells us that when he had done things before he knew of Christ
He was ignorant, meaning he was not a Believer
However, once saved by Christ
He no longer desired to do these things
Now we all know that things happened, and he did not always make the right decisions
But he desired to be whatever it was that God wanted him to be
This is the promise for today
You see what sets us, Believers, apart from the world is our profession of faith in Christ
Our belief that He died for us
That He conquered sin and death for us
But I ask you
Why are so many Believers, Christians, God-fearing people; still living by the standards of the world?
Well, you see, the Lord knew that the physical world in which our fleshly bodies reside would in fact work its way into the spiritual bodies of many of His children
Not that God wants His children to fall victim; however, in war there are always casualties
The question is, what kind of casualty are you going to be?
Are you someone who was born in sin, but accepted Christ?
Or are you someone who was born in sin, sort-of-accepted Christ, until you disagreed with His teachings, and then you rejected Him
You see, a polite no, is still a NO!
If you are the first casualty, then you have a shot at redemption
If, however, you are of the latter, I pray for your soul
Just as a sin is judged as a sin, whether it be a lie, or adultery
Whether it is stealing or murder
Whether it is the swearing on the Lord's Name
In all cases this is a bad thing
And you wonder why I ask, "Have you lost your mind?"
You've lost your mind if you think you can truly be a disciple of Christ
Yet you can hold on to the ways and wisdom of the world
When you came to Him, He made you a new creature
This means that you will, and you must, give up the things of the world
Whether it be cursing, clubbing, fornication, substance addiction, hatred, anger
And anything that the world lives by
You should desire Him first and foremost

You should cast your burdens on Him
As He instructed you to do
Whether you understand or not, He has already taken the burden from you
But, since you are so used to carrying all that weight,
You remain in the same physical and spiritual position
You remain struggling because of yourself
You say that you believe
Yet you still want to do it your way
You cannot do it like that if you truly believe in Him
Psalms 55:22 tells us to, "*Cast thy burden upon the Lord, and He shall sustain thee: He shall never suffer the righteous to be moved*"
This scripture is telling us that we must give the burden to God
If it is a burden that we came to Him with
We must give it to Him
If it is a burden that we picked up along our walk with Him
We must also give it to Him
But the best part of the verse to me is when it says "*He shall never suffer the righteous to be moved*"
This means, if you know that you are called to do HIS work and there are obstacles placed in your way
You are simply to stand in the face of adversity because HE does not want you to move
He will test you
But HE won't tempt you
The enemy will tempt you
But he won't test you
I ask you, have you lost your mind?
You see, a lot of the time we get confused about what we are dealing with
If we seek the wisdom of and knowledge of the LORD
What HE gives us will be worth so much more than we could ever obtain for ourselves
Solomon asked for an understanding heart and the Lord answered him
1 Kings 3:11-12 "*And GOD said unto him, Because thou hast asked this thing, and hast not asked for thyself long life; neither hast asked riches for thyself, nor hast asked the life of thine enemies; but hast asked for thyself understanding to discern judgment;*
Behold, I have done according to thy words: Lo, I have given thee a wise and an understanding heart; so that there was none like thee before thee, neither after thee shall any arise like unto thee"
You see, we always ask God for things to help us out
We are always focused on what we need, instead of what others need
Even Job understood that his focus should not be on himself
Even after losing his children, his property
And being afflicted with sores from head to toe

But he prayed for others instead of praying for himself
The Lord knew his heart and then he was blessed with a double portion
Of what he had originally
You see, God gives us the best all the time
But we, on the other hand, have lost our minds
We give God what we feel like giving Him
We give Him our burdens
He gives us life
We give Him our troubles
He gives us the ability to walk through them
We give Him our complaints
He gives us a voice to pray to and praise Him
We turn from Him when we do wrong
He gives us the ability to return to Him
We wonder about what He wants for us
He gave us a book that lays it all out
We get confused
He said, I am not the author of confusion
We sink into our own sins
He provides us with stepping stones
We should be thinking of Him
He is always thinking about us
We're focused on bills
He told us that he would provide
We worry about our hearts
He said that He would fulfill us to the point of bursting
So, the question is still
Have you lost your mind?
If you have a problem, give it to God
If you can't see the end of the road
Let God drive
Follow the instructions
Stop looking out for you
Start looking out for what God wants
Because He's already mapped out everything before you

[Inspired by **Romans 8:5-6** (NIV) *Those who live according to the flesh have their minds set on what the flesh desires; but those who live in accordance with the Spirit have their minds set on what the Spirit desires. The mind governed by the flesh is death, but the mind governed by the Spirit is life and peace.*]

THE STRENGTH IN THE PAGES

Have you ever noticed how thin the pages of the Bible are, yet the Bible seems to go on forever?
I have a Bible that was given to me in the year 1995. The spine of that Bible has come loose but the pages seem to be just as they were when I originally received it.
This simple concept is important for us all to see and understand. Why? Because the Bible is what? The Bible is the Word of God. The Word of God brought everything into existence. From the beginning there was only God. Remember, God is a Tri-Fold being. So, when I say God, I'm speaking of the Father, the Son, and the Holy Spirit. Now, God decided to give the Son a physical body to sacrifice so that we, the corrupted, sinful, twisted-natured creatures, could have a chance to be redeemed and to come to Him and be saved. Now, in the Garden of Eden, the Son had a physical form, it was the Tree of Life. This was the tree that man chose not to eat from, because of the deception of Satan. You see. that tree in the Garden of Eden has so much significance. Let me break it down for you. We know that the Tree of Life gives eternal life according to the Word of God.
We know that God is not a liar. We know that carpenters take the trees and make them useful. But there are many occupations that require a bit of carpentry. A house cannot be built without a frame. The frame is what everything rests upon. Boat engineers, back in the day, originally used wood to build fleets of ships. Noah used wood to build the ark, which the Lord instructed him to do.
Also, we need to understand that wood, is very important
It can be fashioned to do so many things.
When you injure your leg, they normally give you a crutch made of wood
This is something to help you!
The Ark was created to help man
You see, if not for the wood used in the ark, mankind would not be here; better yet,
If not for God's instructions to Noah, no men, women or children would have survived the flood
Now to bring you to the present day . . .
Wood is important . . .
Wood is used in the creation of paper
Paper is used in the crafting of our Bibles
Our Bibles are printed on paper
There is strength in the pages of your Bible
You see, the pages are the Word of God
You see, the Word of God was given a physical form, Jesus!

Whom showed strength while going through the process for His death on the cross.
He could have asked His Father for 12 legions of angels to rescue Him from the hands of those who would kill Him but, He demonstrated strength
He asked His Father, if it was possible for the cup to pass from His hand
When His Father's will was clarified, He prayed to Him three times
He showed the strength of His faith in the will of God
You see the Word, living amongst us, must have been a glorious thing
But now, we have the Bible, we have that same Word that walked and talked with us
We have that same Word that healed and delivered, we have that same Word that cast out demons from the temple that is man, we have that same Word that loved us and gave His life for us
That Word is our Bible and there is strength in the pages
Have you ever noticed how everything except the pages seem to be the worse for wear?
Have you ever noticed how much your Bible costs at the store?
The Bible is the only book on record, that can never be surpassed in book sales
There is strength and value in the pages
If you are sad, the goodness of the Lord should bring a smile to your face
If you are struggling, the Word can provide you with understanding so that you may find the strength to move forward in your battle
You must understand that in order to accept the strength in the pages, it is necessary to make them a part of your life
Just as eating, sleeping and working is a part of your life
However, you should make it the greatest part of your life
It should take precedence over your life
This is not to say that you should not eat
Only, that there are times when you should fast
This is not to say that you should not sleep
But you should not fall asleep during your prayers to God
This is not to say that you should not work
But when you do work, you should always perform as if you are working for God.
Do your best, as you are His representative
When you are tempted by the enemy, you must seek instruction from the Bible, you must seek strength in the pages to resist that temptation
When you are frustrated, and your tongue is on the verge of releasing a fire that can destroy the will, the spirit, and the drive of your fellow man
You must turn to the Word of God and bridle your tongue
There is strength in the pages
There is strength in the pages
The pages are the remnant

The representation of the life, death, and resurrection, the passion and power that is Christ
So, whenever you need strength, please remember: There is strength in the pages.

[Inspired by meditation on **Isaiah 40:29** (NIV): *He gives **strength** to the weary and increases the power of the weak.*]

PARTING THOUGHTS

To you the reader, I hope that this has provided you some meat to sink your teeth into. As a Believer, we daily face many things that the enemy has put into place (his plots and plans) to steal our joy, to kill our spirit, and destroy our opportunity for salvation. Our one duty is to fortify the spirit within us. We must feed that spirit the Word of God through study, prayer and meditation on the Word of God. We should keep a record of the subjects and people that we pray for, so that when God moves, we can recognize, acknowledge and praise God for what He has done.

We can use this record to help encourage other Believers, some new and even some well-seasoned in the faith. We all grow weary in our journey on this side of heaven. We all need encouragement, from the pulpit to the pew to the pedestrians outside of the church. This record is part of our testimony about the goodness of God to the Believer and the unBeliever. We are supposed to be ready in season and out of season to be a stepping stone and not a stumbling block to any brother or sister in need. I pray that this work, diminutive as it may be, provides you a framework on which to build your own faith.

God bless you and thank you for taking time out of your life to partake.

Adair Rowan, Believer in Christ, son, brother, nephew, cousin, uncle, husband and father.

MWCP & MEDIA LLC

MWCP News & Media

WE ARE A MEDIA COMPANY...

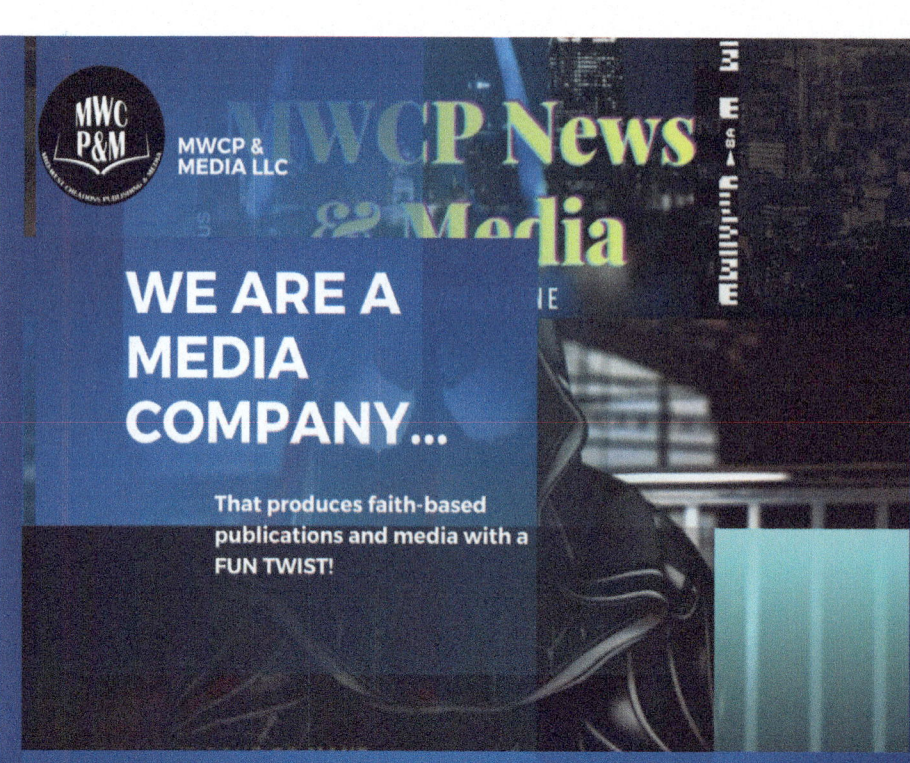

That produces faith-based publications and media with a FUN TWIST!

Affiliate organizations, producers, and sponsors include: Integrity First Insurance, Higher Level Ministries, F-Con Construction and Concrete, The Esther Generation Sister Circle, Saint Jones Productions, Adauro Photography, Praya Wear, and M. Renae Ministries.

SERVICES

Publishing
We help faith-based authors and organizations publish professionally polished works.

Media
We invest and partner with radio broadcasts, podcasts, indie faith-based hip-hop artists, influencers, and more!

Events
We host FAITHCON - a faith-based publishing and media conference every September.

ABOUT US

We are a young faith-based publishing and media company on the rise with big dreams of changing the world by making FAITH fun again.

WHERE ARE WE?

You can find us at our website, on faceBook, Instagram, TikTok, and Twitter! Just google Midwest Creations Publishing and watch the magic happen!

MWCP&MEDIA WEBSITE
www.midwest-creations-publishing.square.site/

Out now on Kindle and Paper Back… See next few pages for preview…

WEEK
01

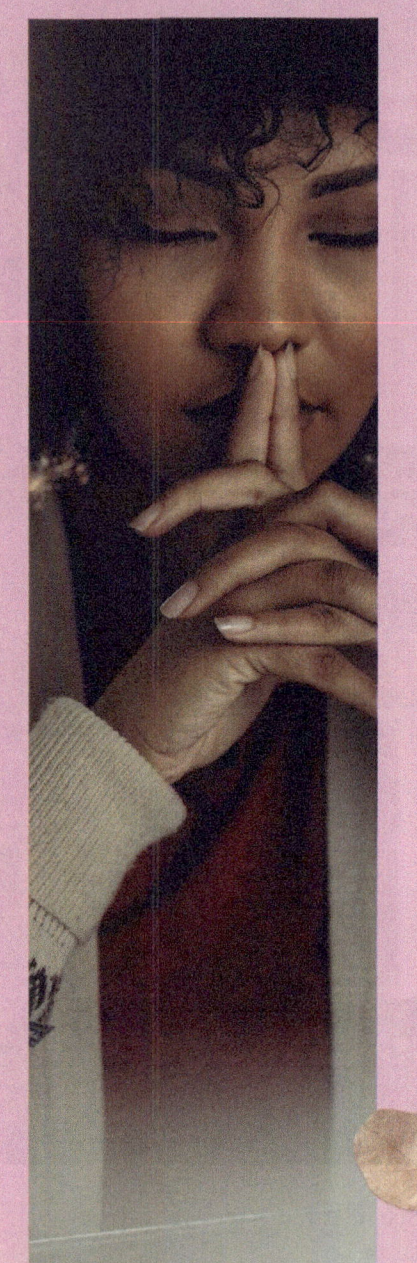

THINK ABOUT WHAT YOU "THINK ABOUT"...

Proverbs 23:7
As a man (or woman) thinks in his (or her) heart, so is he (or she). NIV

LET'S DO IT!

SISTER SQUAD VIBES ✦ WEEK ONE

WALKING OUT MY WEEK
THE PROCESS

THINK IT THRU TUESDAY

Ponder: What thoughts have occupied my time this week so far? Am I anxious, excited, angry, or lethargic? How are my thoughts effecting me?

TALK TO GOD THURSDAY

Set aside at least 5 minutes each time you take a meal today to talk to God about your thoughts. Listen to what He has to say! record your download in Your smartphone notepad.

SITUATION SATURDAY

Look back on your week and think of a specific situation where your thoughts caused (or could have caused) a problem for you and others. How did you handle it? how will you handle it in the future?

SISTER SQUAD WALK IT OUT ✖ WEEK ONE

FEELING
THE VIBE...

VIBING
With God

Vibe with the King of Kings - the lover of your soul! Tell Him how much you need Him to order your thoughts throughout your day EVERYDAY!

VIBING
With your Squad

Text your squad (your family, your girls, or even your work besties) encouraging words to fuel faithful thoughts! Be the change you want to experience!

VIBING
With Self

Take some time out for you this week! A hot bath, sauna time at the gym - wherever you can be alone to vibe with thoughts that refresh your soul!

SISTER SQUAD VIBING — WEEK ONE

YOUR NOTES:

_____
_____
_____
_____
_____
_____

PRAYER:

Holy Father,
In the name of Jesus, let my mind be clear and set on your promises today.

I pray that you will keep me in perfect peace whose mind is stayed on you.

Amen

SISTER SQUAD PRAYER ★ WEEK ONE

MWCP&MEDIA LLC PRESENTS...
Author Chantay M. James'
BRAINWAIVER

Waivering Minds

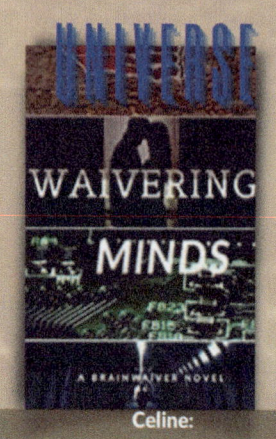

Book I of the Brainwaiver Series

Celine:

A Licensed Clinical Social Worker in Alton, Illinois, Celine Baltimore lives a content, peaceful life. Until one of her patients reveals that her sister has become a guinea pig for behavior modification technology known as "Brainwaiver," then disappears.

Left with a child's journal that paints her once comfortable life in horror and intrigue, Celine finds herself nose deep in corporate secrets, shifty attorneys and rugged, intense men (specifically Enoch Sampson or Sam for short).

Shocked that she's named a winner in the Brainwaiver contest (a contest she'd never entered) Celine learns of more missing children in Alton and their link to the hip new software trying to take over her life; including Sam's teenaged son.

An all-around goof that can't stop tripping over her Aubusson rug (or keep said rug straight) can Celine let go of playing it safe, fight the good fight of faith and get the guy in the end?

Sam:

A widower and ex-CIA agent turned owner of a family owned construction company, Sam picked up a few skills from his former life. Some he wishes he'd never learned. Espionage and secrets had been his business.

Missions and sacrifice had become his life. Growing cold again seemed inevitable... until he met goofy (and determined) Celine Baltimore.

Could he avoid that place of unfeeling and do the unthinkable? Retrieve his son and love again? Because protecting his family was the only thing that mattered to Sam.

It was something that he would do at any cost. It was more than a goal – it was a promise. And Sampson men ALWAYS kept their promises.

Waivering Lies, Book II
the Brainwaiver Series

Max:

Max Arpaio is a Freelance Information Systems Security Analyst and part time Bounty Hunter on occasion. When Max responded to Enoch Sampson's call for help to find his missing son he realized something crucial.

The top government secrets and plots he'd stumbled upon long ago are no longer a shadow on the horizon.

And Now that Denise Ferry has taken up the gauntlet to wage a silent war against Brainwaiver, Max has to make a choice: To help the woman he loves but can never have or stand aside and watch as millions are led like sheep to a slaughter. Either way, he's a dead man. It's only a question of when.

Balboa:

Denise Ferry is a Business Consultant, former FBI agent and a severe pain in Max's rear. A woman who has gone from gang member lieutenant to military strategist to agent, she could write a book on espionage and silent war strategies.

So, when Denise engaged in a search and retrieve mission that targeted children for mind control experimentation, she's in for the long haul to wage war. However, she hadn't counted on warring on two fronts: Against the advances of Brainwaiver and to win the heart of Max Arpaio.

A man of mystery with a sense of doom, Max draws Denise despite her efforts to fight the attraction. Can she help him overcome his dark past?

As a strategist she realizes she has no choice. Without him taking her back against Brainwaiver, she's already lost the war before she starts. And without him in her life she's already lost her heart.

Waiverings, The Anthology
Brainwaiver Universe Novella Collection...

Novella 1.5
Waivering Winds

Novella 2.5
Waivering Times

Delilah and KC's Story:

As Celine's opposition, Delilah did her thing in Waivering Minds, but it wasn't all good... and surprisingly, it wasn't all bad either.

Learn about her horror story compiled of kidnapping, human trafficking and present day slavery.

God and KC have their work cut out for them when it comes to winning Delilah's heart.

But neither one of them is about to give up.

Read her story as God and KC show a woman hurting from the pain of her past that she is more than who she thought she was...

Amanda and Cruz's Story

Amanda, focused on saving the world from Brainwaiver (starting with her mom) finds Cruz irritating... and irresistible.

On a mission from God, Amanda is determined to win her war, and the man that makes her wish she never had to fight one.

However, Cruz Arpaio is no fool. Amanda, at nineteen, was too young for a US Marshall in his mid-twenties.

Not to mention that Denise "Balboa" Ferry-Arpaio, his new and military trained sister-in-law would kill him, if his brother Max didn't first.

So, Cruz left as he was told.

Years later, he still can't get the thought of Amanda Same out of his mind.

Determined to return for the woman he knows is his, Cruz never makes it to his destination.

What happens next turns the worlds of Amanda Same and Cruz Arpaio on its head; and kicks off the war that had been a long time coming.

Will Cruz and Amanda find each other again and somehow, reunite and reignite the powerful attraction that both of them can't forget in these Waivering Times?

Only God knows...

Meet MWCP&MEDIA's...

NEWEST COMPANY

BEST SELLER

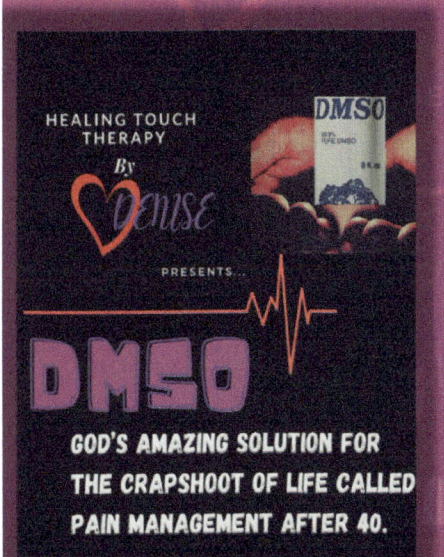

HEALING TOUCH THERAPY By Denise

PRESENTS...

DMSO

GOD'S AMAZING SOLUTION FOR THE CRAPSHOOT OF LIFE CALLED PAIN MANAGEMENT AFTER 40.

BY CHANTAY M. HADLEY & DENISE JOHNSON
LCSW

Available on Amazon
Kindle, Paper and Hardback!
with internationally sold copies in the UK, Spain, France and Canada!

DMSO! God's Amazing Remedy!!!

For some reason life after 40 years of age brings changes in the body that include aches and pains, surprise allergies, sickness and disease, or chronic pain. For years we have depended on big pharma and our medical doctors to provide relief. In doing so, the solutions have been untenable- from medications with side effects that far outweigh the benefits to suggestions that surgery is the only solution.

What if God provided the answer to our issues in nature? Homoeopathic remedies have been studied for years and were mankind's first response for medical treatment.

Queue the amazing remedy "dimethyl sulfoxide" or DMSO. In this book we provide a first-hand accounting of three diverse maladies that cause chronic pain and how DMSO changed our lives! Along with our detailed accounts you will find a brief history about DMSO, a list of maladies that DMSO has been known to help, along with dosage instructions, mixture instructions, and care suggestions.

Enjoy this humorous, and often sad narrative of faith and wellness that transports three women from the ashes of suffering and fatigue to the beauty of relief and peace that makes life worth living again. And maybe... just maybe; you'll find that DMSO is the pot of gold at the end of the rainbow you've been looking for.

Other books by one author, in three different genre's...

Under Pen name: Chantay M. James'

VALLEY OF DECISIONS
A Valley Novel
CHANTAY M. JAMES

Under Pen name: C. Marie Evans

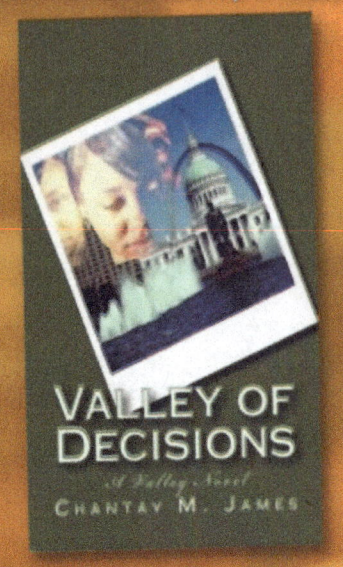

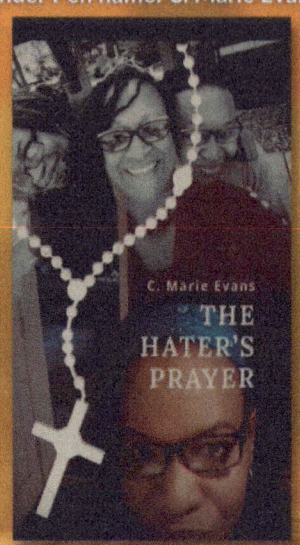

C. Marie Evans
THE HATER'S PRAYER

(Available on Kindle, paperback and on Audible!)

Under Pen names Chantay M. Hadley and C. M. James

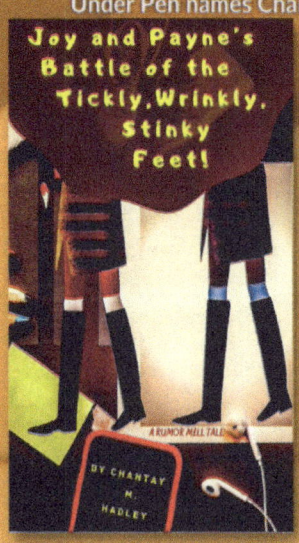

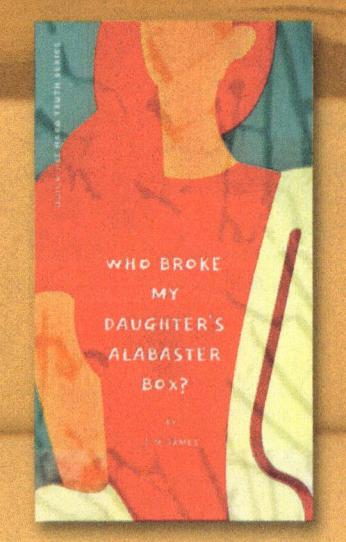

Joy and Payne's Battle of the Tickly, Wrinkly, Stinky Feet!
A RUMOR MELL TALE
BY CHANTAY M. HADLEY

WHO BROKE MY DAUGHTER'S ALABASTER BOX?
BY C. M. JAMES

coming soon...

Under Pen name: Chantay M. James'

WAIVERING EYES
A BRAINWAIVER NOVEL
CHANTAY M JAMES

The Finale! Book 3 of the BrainWaiver Universe

Under Pen name: C. Marie Evans

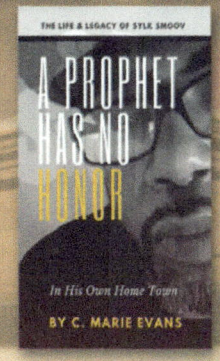

The Hater's Prayer 2: Annie B's Legacy
C. Marie Evans

The Hater's Prayer 3: Legally Bound
C. Marie Evans

THE LIFE & LEGACY OF STLK SMOOV
A PROPHET HAS NO HONOR
In His Own Home Town
BY C. MARIE EVANS

Under Pen Name: C. M. James

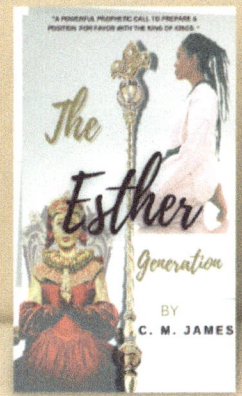

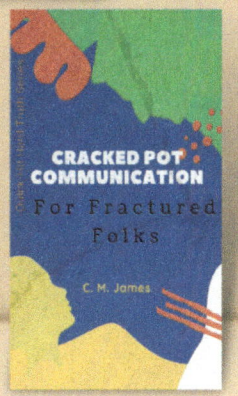

C. M. JAMES
You, The Solution
PURPOSE · PASSION · YOU, THE SOLUTION!

"A POWERFUL PROPHETIC CALL TO PREPARE & POSITION FOR FAVOR WITH THE KING OF KINGS."
The Esther Generation
BY C. M. JAMES

CRACKED POT COMMUNICATION
For Fractured Folks
C. M. James

Made in the USA
Monee, IL
30 March 2023